Hans-Günter Heumann

Piano Junior

A Creative and Interactive
Piano Course for Children
Duet Book 3

ED 13823

Illustrations by Leopé

Mainz · London · Berlin · Madrid · New York · Paris · Prague · Tokyo · Toronto
© 2017 SCHOTT MUSIC Ltd. London. Printed in Germany

ED 13823
British Library Cataloguing-in-Publication-Data.
A catalogue record for this book is available from the British Library.
ISMN 979-0-2201-3650-4
ISBN 978-1-84761-430-9

Cover illustration by Leopé (www.leope.com)
Cover photography: iStockphoto
Cover design: www.adamhaystudio.com
Audio tracks recorded, mixed and mastered by Clements Pianos
Audio tracks performed by Samantha Ward and Maciej Raginia
Printed in Germany S&Co.9214

Contents

Please visit **www.piano-junior.com** to stream or download demo and play-along recordings for all the tunes in the book.

1. A Bogeyman Dances Around in our House

Secondo

German Children's Song
Arr.: HGH

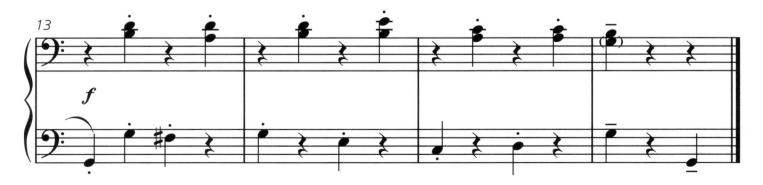

1. A Bogeyman Dances Around in our House

Primo

German Children's Song
Arr.: HGH

2. Dance of the Little Swans

from the Ballet *Swan Lake*

Allegro moderato ♩ = 160

Pyotr Ilyich Tchaikovsky (1840–1893)

Arr.: HGH

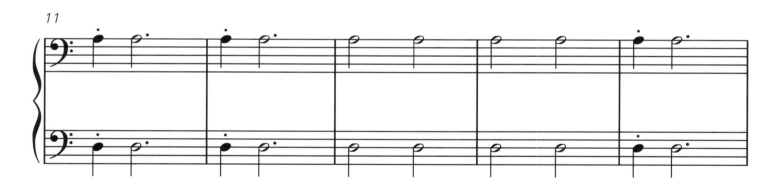

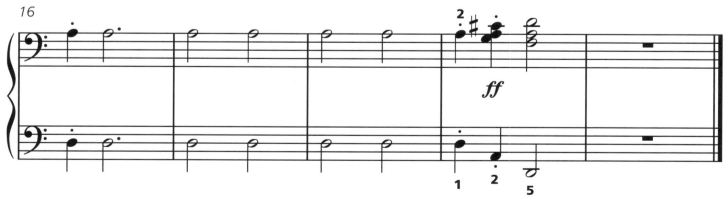

2. Dance of the Little Swans

from the Ballet *Swan Lake*

Allegro moderato ♩ = 160

Pyotr Ilyich Tchaikovsky (1840–1893)
Arr.: HGH

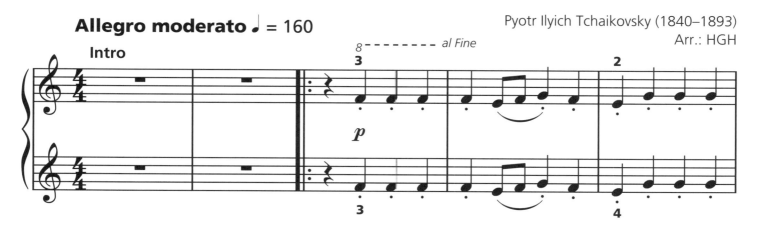

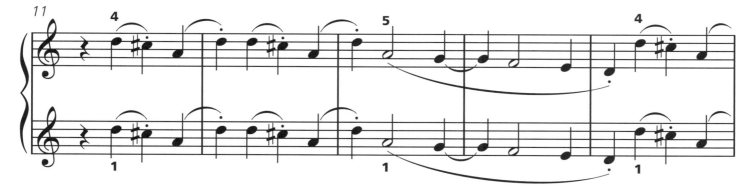

Pyotr Ilyich Tchaikovsky was a famous Russian composer. His works include three well-known ballets: *Swan Lake, Sleeping Beauty* and *The Nutcracker.*

3. The Ice Skaters

Émile Waldteufel (1837–1915)
Arr.: HGH

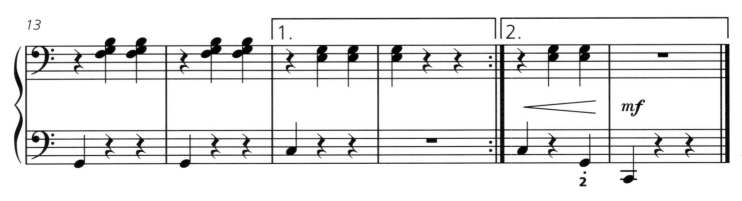

3. The Ice Skaters

Émile Waldteufel (1837–1915)
Arr.: HGH

Émile Waldteufel was a French composer, conductor and composer. He wrote over 250 dances, many of them waltzes.

9

4. Anvil Polka

Albert Parlow (1824–1888)
Arr.: HGH

♩ = 88

Intro

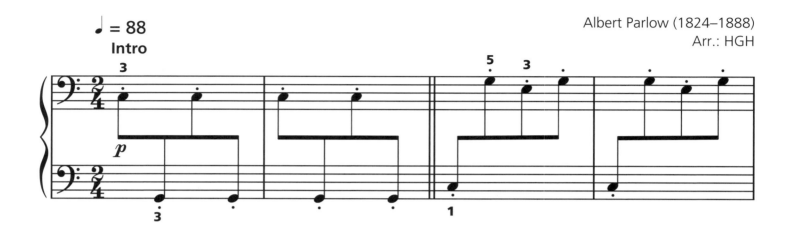

4. Anvil Polka

Albert Parlow (1824–1888)
Arr.: HGH

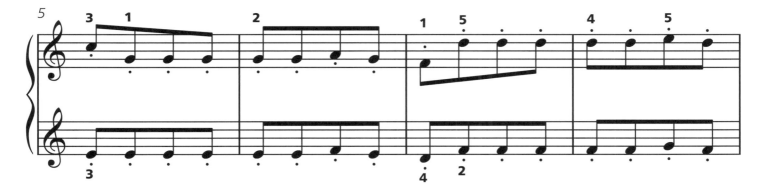

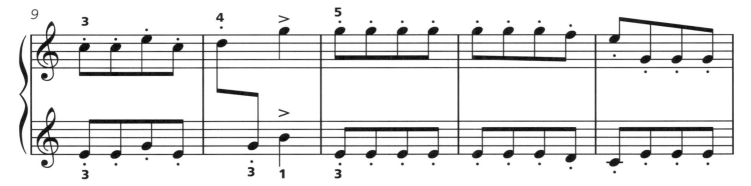

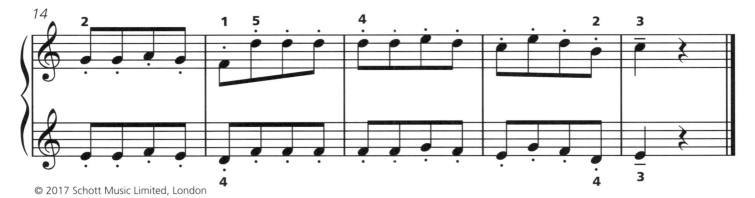

Albert Parlow was a German composer. His *Anvil Polka* became world famous.

11

5. Presto

from *the Musical Children's Friend* Op. 87, No. 35

Heinrich Wohlfahrt (1797–1883)

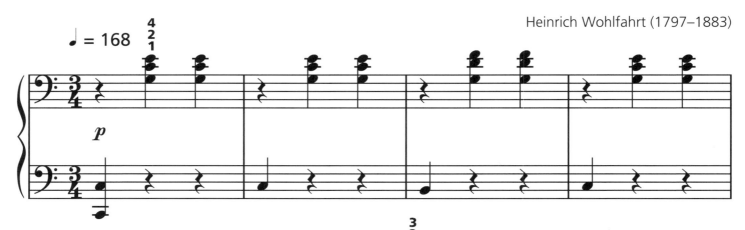

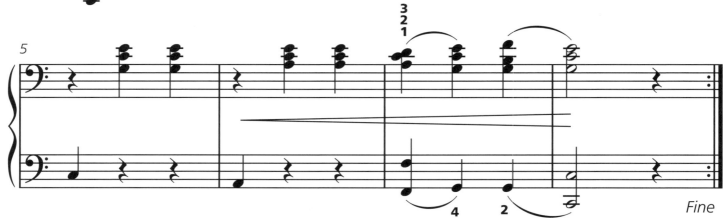

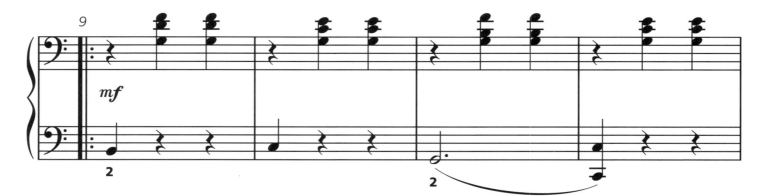

5. Presto

from *the Musical Children's Friend* Op. 87, No. 35

Heinrich Wohlfahrt (1797–1883)

Fine

D. C. al Fine

Heinrich Wohlfahrt was a German composer and piano teacher. He wrote a children's piano method and numerous tutorial pieces for piano.

6. German Dance

Ludwig van Beethoven (1770–1827)

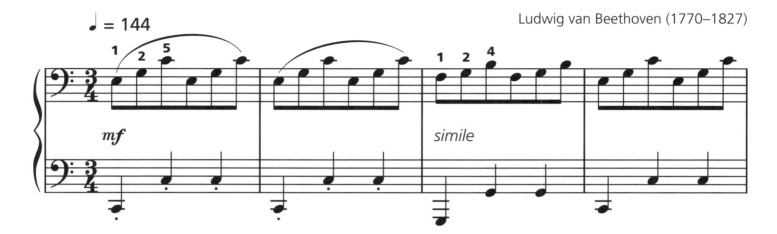

6. German Dance

Ludwig van Beethoven (1770–1827)

 Ludwig van Beethoven was a German composer and a pupil of Joseph Haydn. His virtuoso piano playing and skill as a composer attracted numerous patrons who provided him with financial support. Despite increasing deafness, he still composed great masterpieces.

7. Allegro

Op. 149, No. 4

Anton Diabelli (1781–1858)

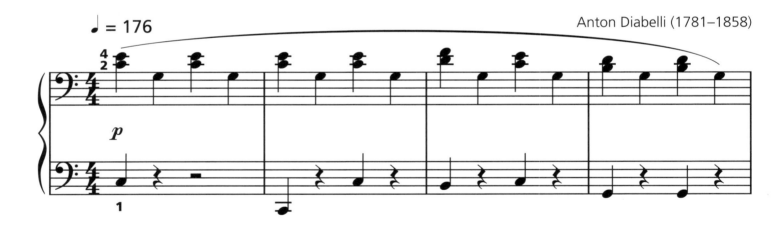

16

7. Allegro

Op.149, No. 4

♩ = 176

Anton Diabelli (1781–1858)

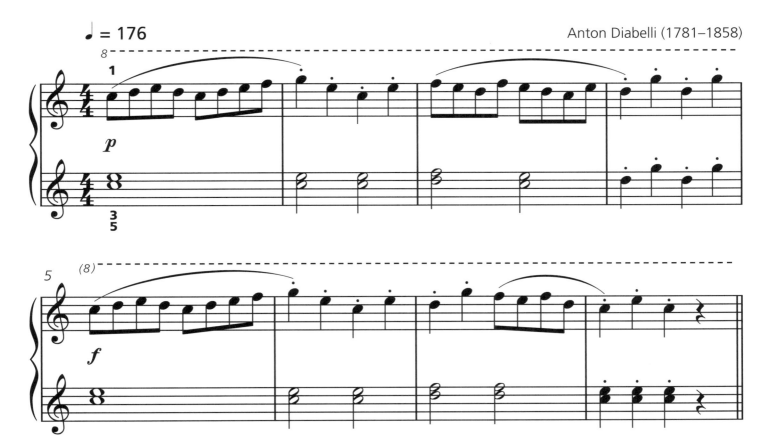

Anton Diabelli was an Austrian music publisher, music teacher and composer.
His *Melodic Exercises.* Op. 149 remain popular for piano tuition to this day.

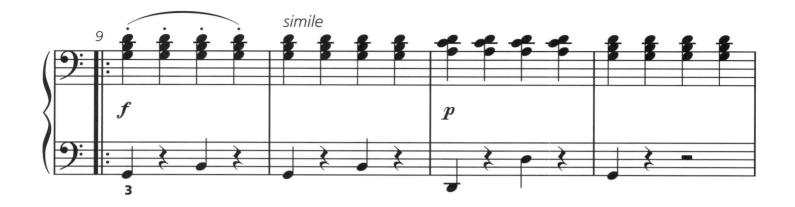

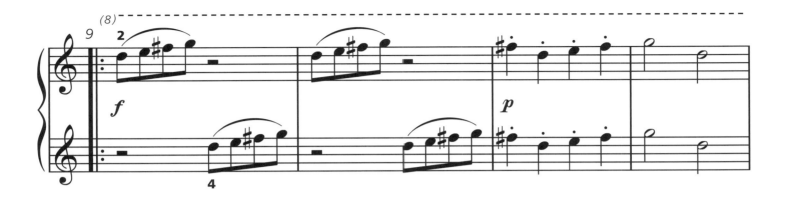

19

8. Once Upon a Time

Espressivo ♩ = 80

HGH

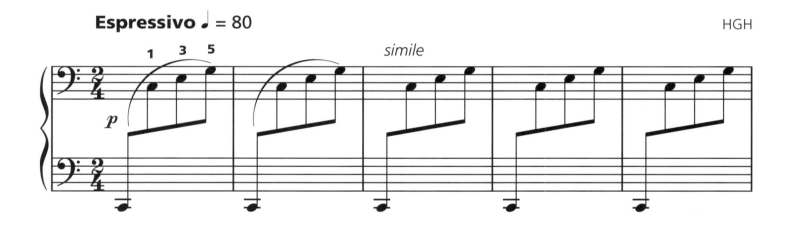

6

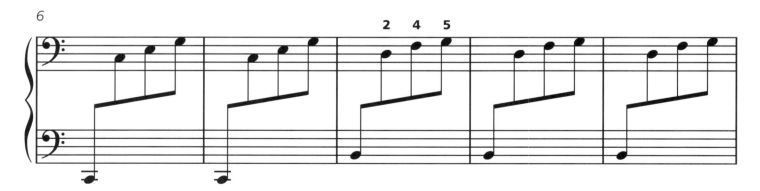

8. Once Upon a Time

HGH

Espressivo ♩ = 80

*) breath mark = take the hands off and go to the next hand position

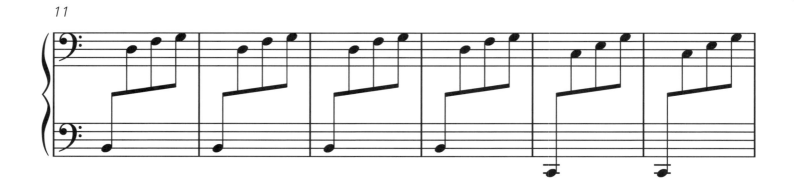

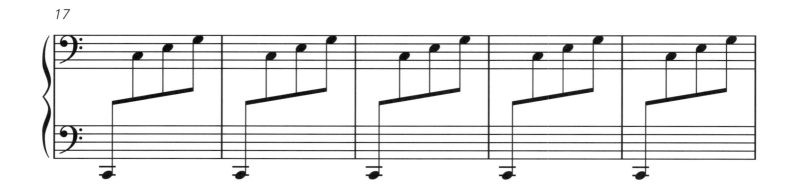

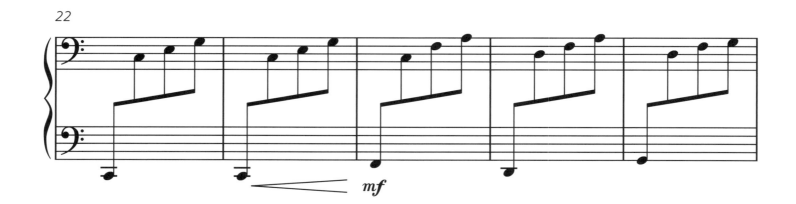

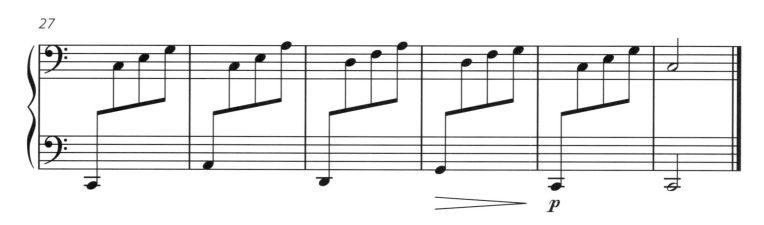

9. Haunted House

♩ = 152

HGH

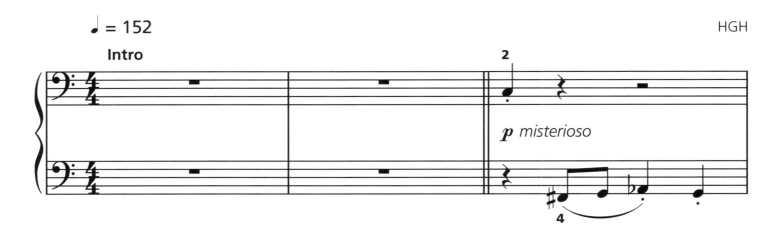

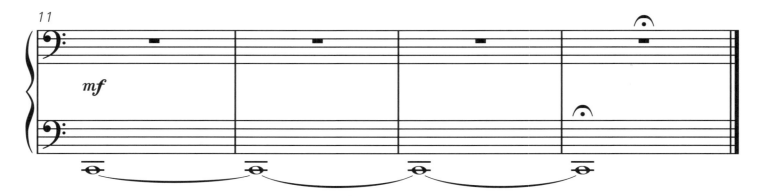

9. Haunted House

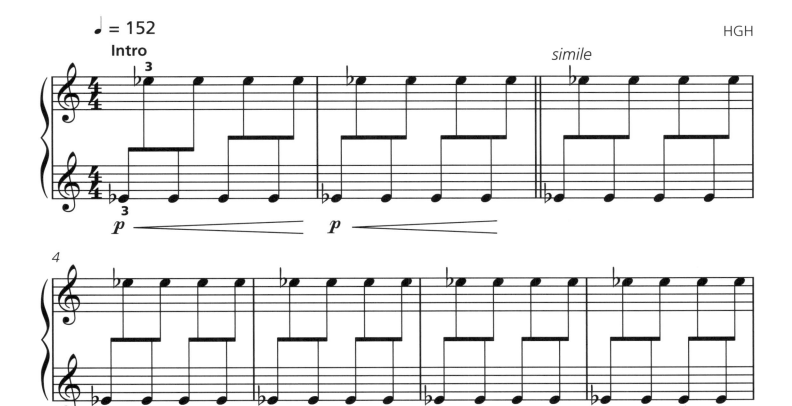

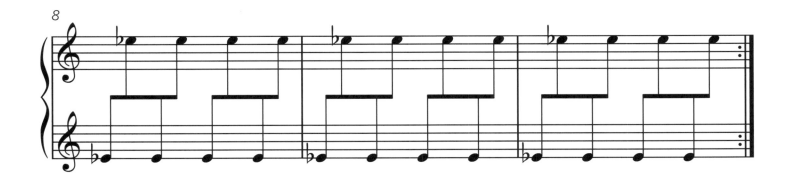

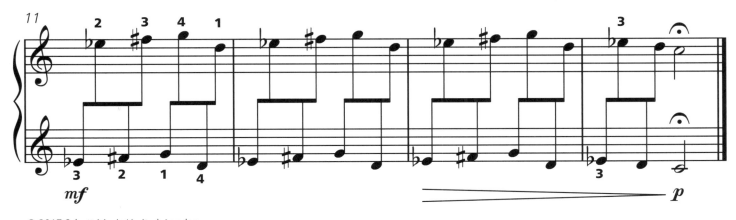

10. Walking Blues

10. Walking Blues

11. Rock That Beat

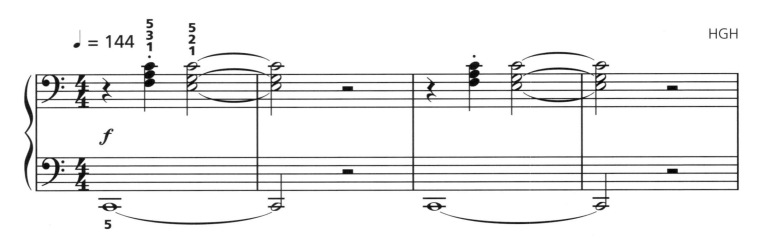

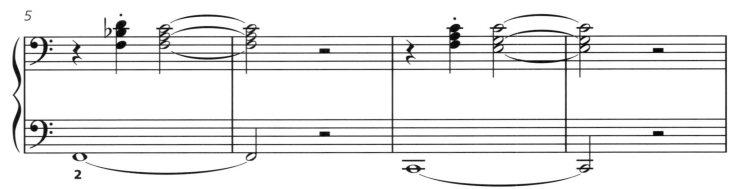

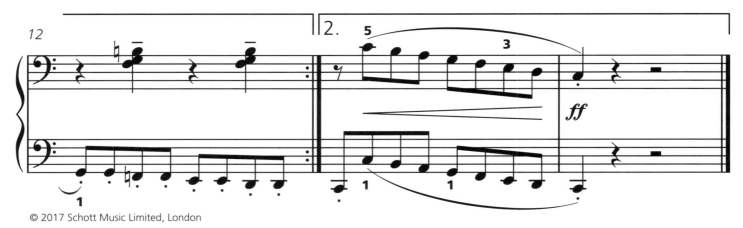

11. Rock That Beat

♩ = 144

*) When the sign *15⁻ ⁻ ¹* or 15 ᵐᵃ (ital. quindicesima) appears over a note or group of notes, play the notes two octaves higher than written.

12. Ländler

Franz Schubert (1797–1828)
Arr.: Johannes Brahms (1833–1897)

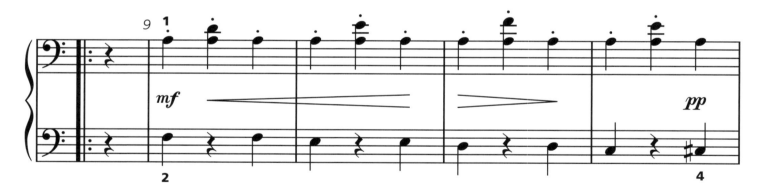

12. Ländler

Franz Schubert (1797–1828)
Arr.: Johannes Brahms (1833–1897)

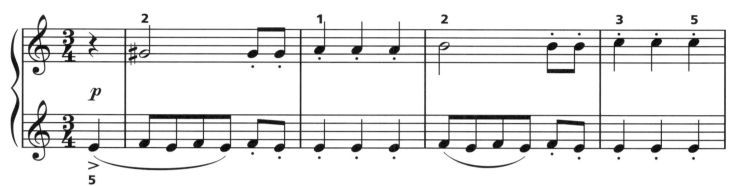

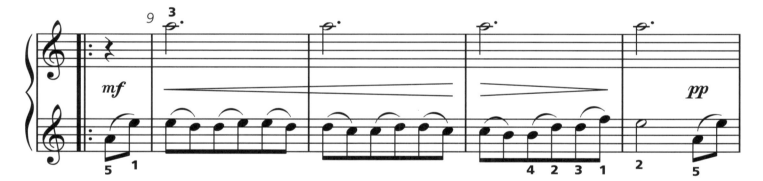

Franz Schubert was a famous Austrian composer. He liked to write music for a small circle of like-minded friends – musicians, painters and poets – who called their musical soirées *Schubertiaden*.

13. Children's Piece

Op.182, No. 5

Carl Albert Löschhorn (1819–1905)

Tempo di Valse ♩. = 60

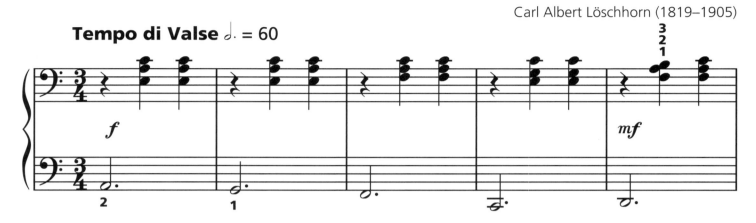

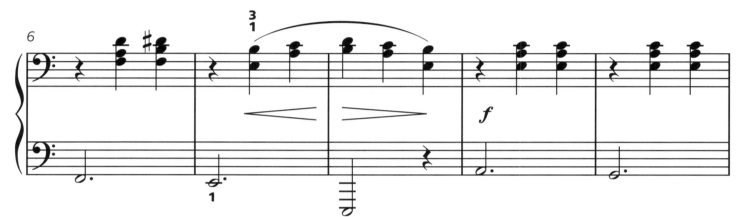

13. Children's Piece

Op.182, No. 5

Tempo di Valse ♩. = 60

Carl Albert Löschhorn (1819–1905)

Carl Albert Löschhorn was a German composer, pianist and piano teacher.

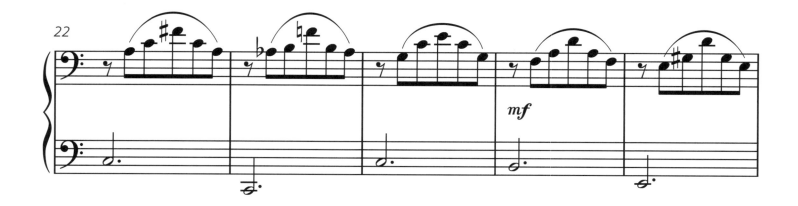

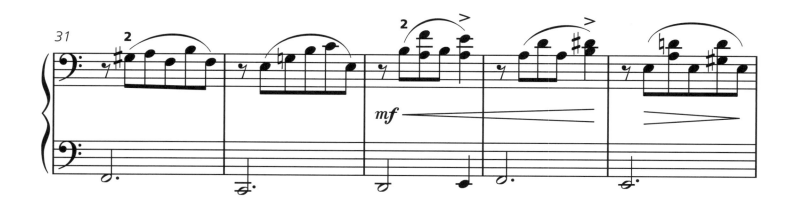

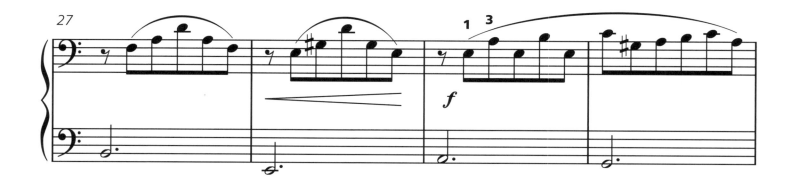

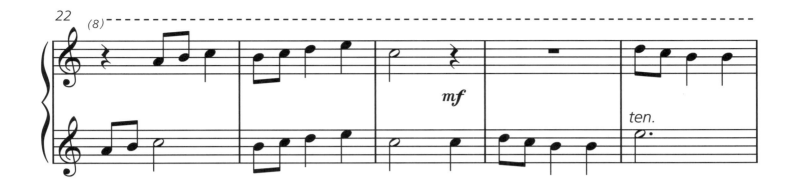

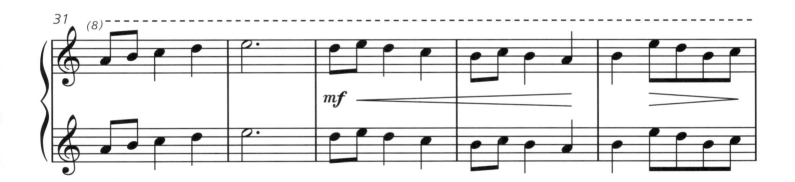

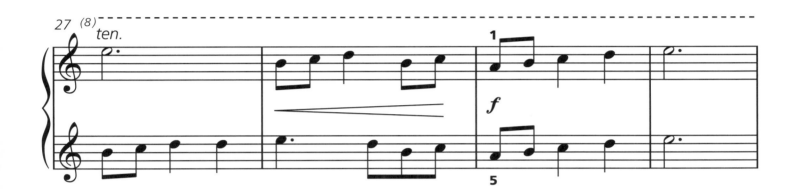

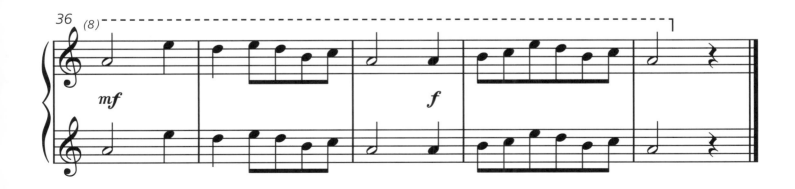

14. Hungarian Dance No. 5

Johannes Brahms (1833–1897)
Arr.: HGH

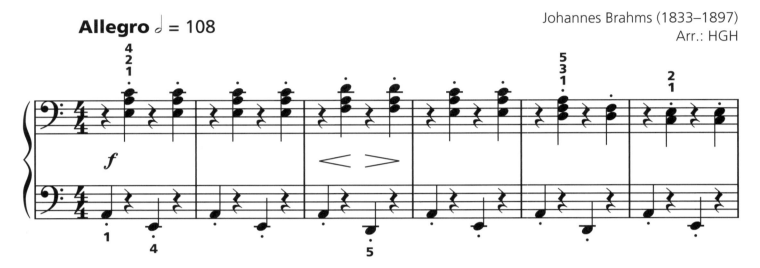

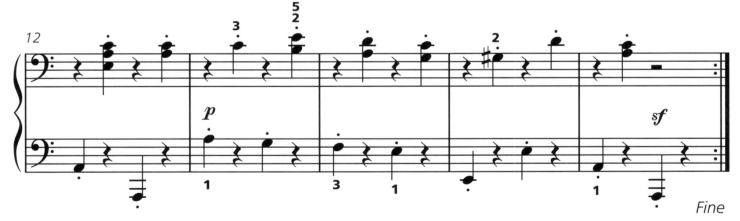

Fine

14. Hungarian Dance No. 5

Johannes Brahms (1833–1897)
Arr.: HGH

Allegro ♩ = 108

Fine

Johannes Brahms was a famous German composer, pianist and conductor. He was a close friend of the composer Robert Schumann and his wife Clara, a celebrated concert pianist. Brahms's best-known works are the *Hungarian Dances* and *Cradle Song*.

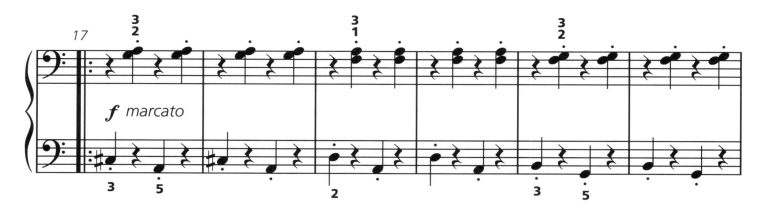

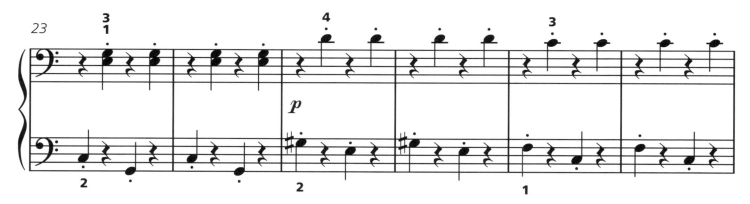

D. C. al Fine

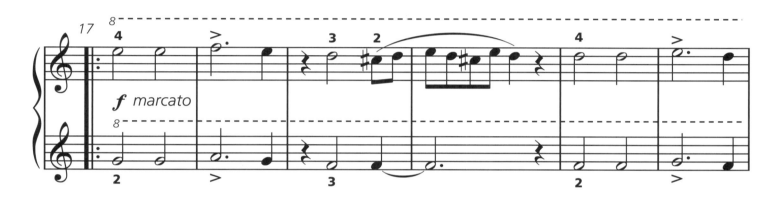

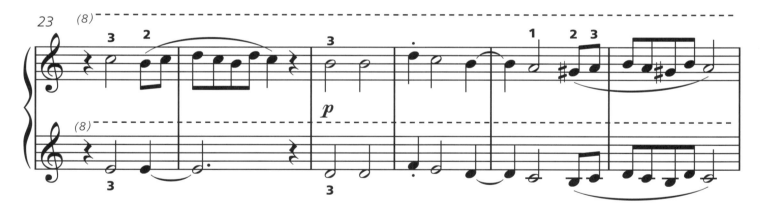

D. C. al Fine